# Explode your Growth!

## Principles for Building Your Team

Coach Dr. JAG

## Dedication

To all those that have encountered struggles in building or repairing their credit after an event, circumstance or life transition.

To all that have chosen to borrow against their future to live a life in the immediate.

There is a hope. There is a future without insurmountable debt

Disclaimer 1

All characters, events, and circumstances are fictional. Any similarity to persons living or deceased are purely coincidental.

Disclaimer 2

This book has been edited multiple times. There are possibly grammatical or spelling errors. While we have edited, revised, and scrutinized, mistakes may exist. If you wish to let us know you found one (or more), please contact me at coachdrjag@gmail.com, providing page number and paragraph, what the mistake is and what it should be. If necessary a revision will be made.

Books by Coach Dr. JAG:

The Core 4 Life Management System

The Core 4 Life Management System workbook.

Foundations in Coaching

The Coaching Manual.

WAH and Other Lame Excuses

The Purge

Implementing the Leader Relationship

Investing in Wealth Building: The Journey from Penny to Wealth

Investing in Wealth Building: The Journey from Penny to Wealth Workbook

Social Media Stimulation: 10 Powerful Tips for Social Networking Success

Climb any Mountain

The Power of the Acorn: A lesson to grow your organization

The Parable of the Diner: A lesson on community

When Good Credit Goes Bad: A story of building solid credit

Explode Your Growth! Principles for growing your team.

1

Noise filled the large room with very high ceilings and open vaults. The half-cubicle walls filtered some of the loud white noise that created intense buzz throughout the room. One wall had a very large monitor showing product offerings, product sales, team sales numbers agents taking calls, the top three sales agents for the current month and last 12 months.

The buzz was constant. The pressure was high. On a side wall in big bright lights were the bottom two teams and the bottom two performers. The high pressure of working in a high volume inbound sales call center was not as glamorous as the hiring representative had made it sound.

Carrie six months ago was sitting in 5th period Biology sitting next to Steve her boyfriend. After school they would go to the coffee and smoothie bar just off campus where they would hang out before track practice started. Carrie, reflected for a moment. Those days were a lifetime ago. The friends she hung with graduated and they all went their separate ways. Well most, Carrie had stayed.

Bill and Carrie were going to go to the state university a few hours away. They had planned this since Sophomore year. He left. She had to stay. A few months later, came the text. He broke up with her over text.

Carrie's father had been in a workplace accident and was on disability. Her college dreams pretty much ended the day her dad got hurt. She had to help with the family income until either dad was back on his feet or a settlement was reached. Carrie had two younger sisters. She had to help care for them as they were 1 and 4 years younger than her. Mom worked 2 part-time jobs. The medical and legal bills were significant. The money did not go far enough.

The career fair at the high school had offered low end, low pay jobs. Many of the fast food places sent reps. She already worked part time at a national franchise. She had for about 3 years. When she saw an opportunity to move to an office position with benefits answering phones and simple service calls for about twice minimum wage, she inquired. The rep was very professional looking and carried herself well. She had an on the spot interview and had been hired based on a verbal agreement. She would work a few hours 3 weekdays per week and Saturday all day until she graduated. She maintained her fast food job as an assistant manager as a fall back.

She started answering basic phone calls. The service calls were generic and pretty basic sending return labels or tracking items being shipped to the customer or from the customer. She did not really get complaints as that was a different call center. The office was nice. She worked on the ground floor of a small office complex on the edge of a corporate and industrial park. The second floor was the entrance for customers. The first floor had its own entrance from the employee parking garage. Call center employees did not get access to the other floors.

Carrie did not complain. She was friendly and courteous on the phone and with her colleagues. She graduated high school about a month after starting the job. The team brought in a cake and flowers for her. She liked the people she worked with.

At her 3-month evaluation she received high marks. She was given a slight bump in pay for completing probation. Her HR rep that conducted the evaluation with Carrie's supervisor. She asked about Carrie's career goals. Carrie stated she had planned to go to college until six months earlier when her dad got injured and could not work.

She stated she was not sure of a career but maybe something in business. She enjoyed this job. Maybe she could learn marketing or sales. Maybe if she was really fortunate she could become a supervisor or manager.

Her supervisor sat back. The HR Rep leaned forward. Carrie do you have a resume? Carrie smiled, what is a resume. The rep explained a one-page document with her education and experience on it. Carrie said No, I do not have anything like that. The rep smiled, you might want to consider one a smart young woman like you. The goals you desire will require one.

The HR rep smiled. Carrie tell me a little about yourself. Carrie gave her a verbal run down of work experience, her education, and her family. She explained about mom working two jobs, dad being unable to work, and her two younger sisters. The rep smiled.

Carrie, the HR rep stated, you seem like a smart girl. You might be able to do me a favor. We recently had an opening in our inbound call center. I think you would be a perfect fit. The supervisor said nothing and had been shuffling through the files for the next interview. The rep continued. The hourly rate is a little less though you will make extra money for every product or service you are adding to a customer's account, we call that a commission.

As you add enough services to accounts, you can make a bonus on top of that. If you add specific services or products you can make a larger commission. So, while the hourly rate is less, you can make so much more. Some of our people make over $100,000 per year. Carrie brightened up. What would I have to do? The rep smiled.

We will train you. There is a short training course. You will be talking to customers about products and services. You will share the added value of these items and how it will make their life or service better. When they agree, while you are talking to them, you make some money for telling them.

We could spend it on a large marketing campaign with a big company. Our company wants to help our people to be successful. We offer the option to our people to make an above average paycheck for telling people about our company and our products. What do you say?

Carrie smiled. I would like to make a better paycheck. The rep smiled. Of course, you would. You are smart as this will make you a full-time employee. One of the perks is we pay for college tuition at a few online universities. If the degree is in a field that benefits the company such as business, marketing, project management, or production we offer a full tuition for a 7-year commitment. This translates to 4 years for the degree and 3 years' experience afterwards. If you decide to leave after this, there is no cost to you. If you leave before the 7 years is up, you repay a prorated amount for the tuition. Are you interested in the program?

Carrie smiled. You mean I can get my degree and work experience? The rep chuckled of course. It is a win for everyone right? Carrie signed the contract. That had been a Friday. She would start on Monday in training.

2

Carrie strolled into the training room around 7 on Monday morning. She headed to a relatively dark corner in the back. She hid mostly behind the workstation. She looked through the binders that were mostly empty sitting next to the workstations. She found the logins to get access on the workstation. Nobody else was in the room at the time. She decided it would be better to work from her phone and write down some ideas as to what might be reasonable goals under the new job. She was not sure what to expect.

She had been very excited on Friday. Over the weekend she became increasingly nervous and anxious about the new position. As the clock slowly wound up towards 8 o'clock, more people began to stream into the training room. She did not want to talk to anyone else in the room. Many faked looking busy working in the notebooks. Others got on their phone or tablet devices to avoid choosing to be interacting with others. Another young woman such as Carrie took the other side of the back row in the corner. She tried to disappear. Carrie tried to jot down some thoughts that she had about the organization and this new position. What could it mean?

At 8 AM sharp, the trainer took the last swig of her coffee and started the training. She introduced herself and went over some basic premises of how the training would be structured. She explained the purpose, the mission, and the vision of the organization.

She then explained vision and mission with the corresponding objective of the call center in which this training was focused. This training was intended to make better call center representative in order to achieve great results. Greater results meant more resources for the company. Committing more resources, greater results were in evitable. Sales and service to maximize profitability and potential while providing extraordinary service. This training is not for everybody. Find the system that works for you. We will lay out a structure in which we expect you to follow. It is up to you to find a flavor that works best for you.

The class took the next hour or so briefly introducing themselves and what their initial goal was individually for being in the position. Carrie quickly learned, money was a strong motivator for most of her colleagues in the training. Carrie briefly introduced herself and stated that she had an eagerness to learn, though she wasn't really sure how she would do or what she was going to be doing. She stated she had a couple months of experience working at the service center working inbound calls. She quickly learned that pretty much everybody in there in the training was from a similar situation.

Just after the midmorning break, the trainer I placed a large packet of papers at each workstation. She stated they would begin working through these packets as he's over the policies and procedures for working in a sales call center. As she began to work through this, she began to talk about having a goal. Part of this process is knowing who you are and what you bring to the table. What is the benefit in value that you bring to the organization? What is the value and benefit the organization brings to you. The relationship must be some biotic and mutual

Carrie made a note of this. She often thought of herself as timid and shy. She knew that nervousness or anxiety was not going to give her success. If she wanted the bonuses and a better paycheck she would have to change. Fear was not an option. She saw many not really paying attention to the trainer, doing their own thing.

The trainer began with an exercise. She asked each individual to open their notebook, write down their immediate work experience and a career objective within their current position as they understood. This exercise took about five minutes. She stated to write a one-page synopsis of these experiences and how they have led to getting wherever you are today. Carrie thought about this, and that her job at the fast food restaurant had not really given her a lot of experience, or so she thought. As the trainer went around the room she learned many others also had more experiences.

Working in food service or very blue-collar establishments had provided problem-solving skills, understanding the dynamics of teamwork, customer service skills, or time management and a host of other skills that she had not been aware of. Many people, stated they think that working in quick food service is dead end. What you choose to do with it is up to you.

The trainer added, there are many skills that I learned. When Ray Kroc developed his systems for McDonald's Corporation, he deliberately established an operational system that could be mastered by untrained, and unskilled individuals working together for success. The system still works almost 70 years later. The dynamic has not changed though some of the processes have. We must learn to overcome and adapt to new needs. The same is true in this new position.

Someone saw something in you to believe you would be successful in this position and might've been the human resources representative, or it might've been yourself or colleague prodding you to take the next step. Now it is time to consider what are you willing to do to step up and step out to achieve at a far higher level? Carrie began to think about this and jot some notes. She began to look at her work experience in a slightly different way.

Many people would say she was in dead end, entry-level jobs. She would say she is begun in training programs that can take her to greater levels if she would continue to work it. Developing a plan, and working on a plan or two very different things she learned that she listened to the trainer and they begin working through orientation of the corporation in and its purposes in a new way.

Carrie listened carefully as to how the organization was set up and what resources are available for those that were willing to step up and step out. Carrie made a note of this. The trainer suggested developing a plan with career objectives and goals. She talked about the value of training both formally and informally. She talked about the value of getting a good education from an academic standpoint and from a practical standpoint. Being able to bridge academic, with practical is the beginning of wisdom, being able to build on this, deconstruct, then reconstruct an idea, concept, or process becomes invaluable that few will ever fully achieve. It was then that she also talked about having a good mentor and mentoring others bringing it all full circle. Everyone benefits, it is a win-win situation.

Carrie considered what needed to happen for her to change. The trainer spoke of being honest with yourself. She spoke that if you will truly assess where you are at and know where you want to be, the journey to get there becomes clear. Author, Stephen Covey in his book "The 7 Habits of Highly Effective People" says we should begin with the end in mind. If we do not have an end goal, any path will get us there.

The trainer made the comment that doing what we have always done and expecting different results is the very definition of insanity. To create change, we must consider and plan the change then choose to change. Action is required. Talking and thinking will carry only so far. Carrie took many notes and chose to make decisions to create greater change for herself and for her family. She had many ideas, but nothing tangible or actionable currently, that would have to change.

Carrie listened as the trainer spoke more walking through different scenarios. She began to make note of resources within the company and trainings that were available. She began to think of her career in a new way. She made notes of what she could do. She made notes of what the organizations could to do for her.

A big part of this was finding a mentor. The trainer had talked about having a mentor that is at least a few steps ahead of where you are and going where you want to be to learn from. This apparently had great value as she spent much time discussing it. She also took a sign-up sheet for those who would be willing to enter the mentoring program that the company offers. Carrie begin to get nervous of where this is going out of it was all knew it very exciting.

The trainer shared a few success stories. She told the story of a young woman that was fresh out of high school and had no real job experience. The young woman was nervous. She hesitantly found a mentor. The mentor actually scared her at first. The mentor committed to working with her but demanded a lot in return and complete dedication to the improvement and advancement of the individual and their performance. The young girl, intimidated and anxious agreed.

The next two years were rough. It was like a 24-month boot camp. The young girl grew and developed in many areas becoming a confident young woman. She found multiple mentors in key areas of her life. She maintained and grew her relationship with her first mentor. Through her continuous efforts gained promotions and skills advancing beyond many of her peers that were going through the motions. She admittedly decided while the work was hard, it was necessary to lay the foundation.

The young woman built a team of supporters with like mindedness to achieve. When she advanced, they advanced with her. Eventually, she ran her own unit, then a department. Her team's results outshined most comparable teams, winning multiple awards. The team grew, as did their successes.

Ten years of mentoring and being mentored by her original mentor as well as those she had mentored in her team, She and her team built a strong organization. She was offered her own division. In which she grew and advanced the teams, forming teams within the team. The bottom line is this quiet, shy, and timid young teenager became a strong and successful business woman in a relatively short period of time.

The trainer concluded the morning session with: The training this week will lay core foundational process and practices. The organization offers many resources for those willing to step up and step out. What will you choose to do? Will you duplicate this young teenager? Will you work and find it requires more than you are willing or able to give and fall away to pursue other opportunities? The choice is yours. You must decide. Decide soon before circumstances decide for you.

At lunch, Carrie sat with some others from the training and tried to make conversation. She began to ask others what they were getting out of the training. Sharon, the girl sitting on the other side of the room in the other back corner stated she found it very interesting and was very willing to explore this. She was excited. Carrie and Sharon began to talk. Several others stated they didn't see the value in what was being offered it was just an added requirement. They just wanted to make a lot of money. Carrie was not sure she totally understood that. One of her new coworkers in this training said she is a single mom with three kids under age 5. The fathers of her children provided no support whatsoever. It was about the money. It was about what the company could offer her. Carrie thought, it wasn't just what the company could offer her, but what she could offer the company in order to build a greater relationship. That seemed to be a theme by the trainer.

Carrie got back to the training room a few minutes early and had a chance to talk to the trainer privately. She asked if the trainer knew anything about the university and the online university program. The trainer smiled.

She stated she had just completed her MBA specializing in organizational leadership through this program. She made for use of all the educational opportunities formal and informal that the organization offered. Carrie began to think. She asked questions as to how she could gain more information about this. She suspected there were opportunities here, but they would not just come to her. She would have to find them.

The training started off the afternoon. The trainer asked those in the class to pair up with somebody to practice some roll play. Carrie and Sharon found via each other and headed to the corner They worked through some of the scenarios. They talked about plans and the lives in between running the scenario. It turned out they had grown up 20 minutes from each other all their lives. They ran in very similar circles but just different enough that they never ran into each other. Sharon was about a year older.

The trainer came over to them to coach them through scenarios. It became clear there were challenges. The trainer stated while the scenarios are real, there is a greater value in finding your own personality when taking calls. Most representatives need to adapt their personalities of their callers in order to bring about the maximum results. Carrie listened and tried addressing situations as she might with a friend. The trainer warned her that this may work most of the time though not always. If they reject the approach, they are not rejecting you.

Carrie did not fully understand. The trainer shared on the late afternoon break, the organization hires many call center representatives for service and sales. Due to the high volume, only about 20% make it past 90 days before either they transfer or quit. Most will be attracted by the money. Once they realize what is really expected, they struggle. By then it is too late. Carrie frowned a little.

The trainer caught this. She looked at Sharon and Carrie. Ladies, you are young. I am guessing you both have reasons for wanting the job. If I may, set reasonable goals. Do not shoot for the stars as you may be told by your colleagues and superiors. A persistent 10% increase every 31 days is the company requirement. The teams may try for more. Stick with what is expected and do an extra step each day. Once you have that step after a week, add another step. Continue the process of improvement each and every day, each and every shift. You will get there. There is one more thing.

Carrie asked what is the one thing? Build your career. Become the best at what you do. Carrie asked, "how do I do that?" The trainer smiled. "Carrie, there are many ways. My initial thought is closely observe what others are doing and watch their results."

We all make mistakes if we are learning. When we do not make mistakes, we may have become complacent. Risk and succeed also means to risk failing. Watch what works and what does not. Ask questions. Practice your technique, then practice some more. Some may have the right idea though are not executing correct. Others may execute well though are not comfortable. Determine what's new. Work it into your system if it is a good fit. Timing and execution can make the difference. Finally find someone to mentor you, mentor someone else, and find like-minded individuals that have chosen to succeed. If you do this, you will succeed. It may be hard, though the work will pay off.

Training progressed throughout the week. Carrie began building friendships where she could. Others would be colleagues but little association. Carrie on Day 3 brought in a small fruit platter and chocolate chip cookies. She used the food to try and break the ice with those she had not interacted.

Carrie tried to build a relationship with Sharon. She learned more about Sharon's situation. The new position was very important to Sharon, yet she struggled to commit. She needed the money to make a better life for her and her kids. Carrie talked about a career plan as the trainer had said the first day. Sharon talked of what she wanted though would not develop a strong workable plan. She would only speak in ideals. Carrie had spoken to the trainer, Karen about making a career plan.

Karen had shared that many will make a plan. The steps are grandiose and unachievable as laid out. The organization had many resources to assist in the process. There is instructor led trainings onsite and classroom, computer based, and webinar recordings. The HR department had many templates available as well as resource library. Karen stated the leadership strongly believed in the Learning Organization approach allowing training, development, and performance improvement for those willing to step up.

Carrie asked why more people are not advancing in the organization. Karen smiled. We can support and encourage, we can provide the resources, we cannot make them use them. Many will fall off three feet from gold. Carrie asked what does that mean. Karen stated it is a reference to the book Acres of Diamonds. She recommended Carrie read the book.

The training week had come to a close mid Friday afternoon. Carrie stayed after all the trainees had left. She asked Karen if she would be a mentor to her. Karen smiled. Carrie, I have not worked in the call center for several years. Here is what I will do. I will mentor you for professional development. I will give you a lot of reading and assignments. We will go over them and discuss results on a monthly basis. I travel a lot right now. We will discuss over email during the month with a two-hour session Saturday morning at 6am. This should not conflict with either of our work. We will meet the last Saturday of the month unless otherwise arranged. Is this acceptable? If you do not do the assignments, the agreement is off. Carrie agreed. Karen stated there are two other things. By our first meeting find a mentor at the supervisor or manager level in your department that you will learn from. Also find 4 other individuals that also want to actively improve their advancement potential in the field and in the organization. The final item, you must enroll in two classes towards your degree at the online university we contract with. You will be actively enrolled and successfully passing classes for us to continue our mentoring. Are you in agreement? We are agreed. Karen smiled. Carrie, I know it is a lot. You will get tired. I am here for you. It is vital we lay this foundation. You will be successful either here or elsewhere if you stay this course. Carrie smiled. I look forward to the challenge.

She went home excited for the first time in months

Over the weekend Carrie worked on refining her resume. There was not a lot of information on a professional level. Carrie studied resumes, positions and companies in her field. . She looked for ways to bring out more from her knowledge and skills. She accessed many local networking groups as to those in similar fields with similar goals. She stared an online relationship in these groups. She was working on education though did not hold a collegiate degree.

She developed a resume that focused more on specific skills. The balance between formal and informal education is a fine line. Based on conversations she had with peers and supervisors' informal education often comes with practical experience and a degree of investment and learned respect. Even when failing in a task there is a significance in the learning. The formal education provides greater conceptual, theoretical learning through advancing critical and creative thinking skills. The formal learning was beyond being in the moment or situational.

2

Carrie walked into work that first day at her new call center. Her palms are sweaty, she was very nervous as well as anxious about starting the new position. Her excitement, anxiety and nervousness temporarily kicked in. She began taking calls. Some customers were rude and a little more direct. Others did not use such a polite language. Others were extremely kind and patient as she was learning the new system and trying to establish a protocol. She quickly understood the power of relationship as well as adapting to different communication styles. This much she had learned from the training. She quickly learned there was no way for the training to fully prepare her for what she was now encountering.

Carrie quickly learned that earning the minimum commission was not going to get her very far. She further learned, if you will learn to listen and turn phrases, a few compliments in the right place all came at a price. Making the right suggestion at the right time, with the right person could be very lucrative. Her lead taught her, be a problem solver. They have an issue or concern, you have their solution. It is in how and when you present this by making the pain bad enough to want to change.

Over the coming days and weeks, she continued to phone and expand her professional client file. It was through these experiences that she asked questions of those that did well. She observed those that did not. Often success and failure were a very thin line. Timing and delivery was essential. She learned what to say and what not to say. She learned how and when to say things, and when to not say anything at all. Soon she was offered a position to move over to sales and receive this training. Her numbers over a three-month period soared, after getting the basics down. From then on it was expanding on the basics and doing the basics better.

Carrie continued to improve her approach and technique. She met with Karen multiple times. Karen continued to give Carrie several different books to read. She developed her basic skills and adapted quickly to the sales training network. Joseph, her director just said that she apply to the management training program that the company offers. Carrie submitted her application and found several networking groups for young professionals working to improve their situation and meet like-minded individuals.

At these groups she made many contacts and contacts. She met Mike a mentor who offered to help her with her leadership skills as well as allowing her to intern in his firm out as a night and weekend supervisor. He ran a small dispatch company of service professionals. A Commercial & Residential Janitorial Maintenance organization would be a great opportunity. Carrie continued to read as well as study those who have gone before. She began to read some of the great motivators and sales leaders.

Very often these reads, or audios would counter for the attitudes in the call center because she was so frequently surrounded by negative. She quickly learned that maybe 10% of the individuals that work in the call center with her on the service side or on the sales side truly had a good attitude or a desire to improve and advance within the organization for the good of the organization and their own personal success.

Carrie completed several books that she was given as well as she began leading trainings on her own. She began studying sales team development everywhere she went. Whether going to a restaurant or a store for entertainment venue, she would watch how one or two individuals may be a top sales person by offering suggestions, while many others went through the motions and barely even did what was expected. She continued to read on sales as well as communication skills. Karen suggested also that Carrie should begin her education and motivation in leadership by attending seminars, webinars, and biblio-mentoring by many great motivational individuals. For us to improve, we need to study those in the past and those of your profession to continually improve.

Carrie very much enjoyed the reading that she was doing, soaking up the knowledge and wisdom of these professionals in their field. She knew she did not know and that she could better abilities based on those who have gone before learning from their experiences, so she would not have to reinvent the wheel. She continued to talk to many of her like-minded friends and colleagues in order to solidify what she was learning.

She discussed it with some of her friends in her online university courses. Some got it, many did not. We can learn but not everybody would fully understand. The fact was that many would agree, or fewer would ever choose to apply the principles.

She discussed some of these concepts and ideas with her friends who had gone off to college though not really entered the workforce yet as they were wrapping up their freshman year at the University. Carrie had completed a year of experience in several different forums, expanded her network as well as completed several academic goals of her first year using the accelerated courses that the online university offers without the expense requirement for being on campus. She was missing the college experience of dorm wife and the freshman 15, as well as many of the activities and other freshmen were having. She was a commuter student by their understanding and working. She had heard about these things though since she had not experienced them, she did not miss them

Her experience was very different than those of a traditional **university** freshman for a person her age. Carrie learned to work doing what you enjoy. Carrie was willing to go out and get it. She sacrificed some of her young adulthood play that many of her friends were enjoying, by providing for her family. Her father had taken a turn for the worst. Her mom working many hours but also was getting sick from the stringent requirements that were in place on her.

Carrie was motivated to fix these family concerns. She often talked Karen about this. Karen usually responded with, "The smarter you work, the better you will be paired to resolve this situation. You are planting seeds now. It will allow you to take care of this issue in ways that most will never be able to."

Carrie was not sure what that meant that she was placing seeds for harvest that others would never enjoy or understand. Carrie knew that she trusted Karen. Karen had not steered her wrong and had taken her under her wing. Carrie was enjoying some results for all the hard work she was doing. Karen reminded her that she was making sacrifices now for rewards that would far exceed what she could imagine if she would persist and make these changes while continuing to improve and advance in all areas of her life. Balance in all areas with critical. Carrie agreed blindly did not understand but knew there was value.

Carrie's evaluation came due. On the specified day she went to a small conference room where her supervisor, manager, and director were sitting behind the table. They invited her to have a seat for her semiannual review. Carrie took a seat. Her supervisor sang her praises as to the contributions she made for the team. Her manager reported solid numbers that Carrie had accomplished consistently.

The director shared some thoughts as to objectives of the organization. After summarizing and reviewing the various components, the director asked Carrie how she thought she had done this last six months? Carrie spoke to her goals within the organization and her career. Carrie opened her portfolio and shared a chart that she had maintain asked to growth personally achieved and those she was working towards. She shared books that she had read, seminars she had attended, and classes she had completed. She talked of pouring in being a mentor and being mentored.

The manager and director stated they were not aware of her progress. Her supervisor made note of these things. So, you have not shared this information previously with supervisors, the director asked? The manager asked what Carrie's next set of goals were? Carrie shared that she wanted to move over to a different group, under a different supervisor to be mentors and gain experience if possible.

The manager agreed to make that happen as he also thought that would be a good alignment. The director inquired from Carrie as to three things that she has learned from her present team and supervisors over the last six months. Carrie could share some of her observations of what worked well and what had not. She shared where she had been able to improve and make adjustments to get a greater result. The director was very impressed.

The director asked her if she was in the management training program through the organization. Carrie replied that she was in and advancing. She was hoping to gain some other experiences formally and informally as well as begin attending the roundtable discussion session. Carrie shared some of her other leadership experience and opportunities. The director mentioned that there was a new team he was warming for high-performance associates. Would she be interested in trying this on a 90-day basis. If it worked out well she would be offered a permanent position. Carrie accepted the challenge. The opportunity gave her mentoring with the director, put her with other like-minded individuals for success orientation, and learn greater sales and marketing techniques as well as customer service and communication skills. The team would have round table discussions of the brown bag lunches on a regular basis for continuing in-service training.

Carrie was able to apply her skills as well as share in the progress that was being made. The program would empower her to be able to do more. Carrie's evaluation ended on a good note. She gained a $2000 bonus for her merit and continuing service. She received a $1000 bonus for training and verified education Her supervisor and manager signed off on the transfer. She would start with the new team immediately.

Carrie watch her leave the meeting room. She seems frustrated with the situation. Carrie has become a top earner in the group. Supervisor struggled with attitude, personalities, products, and services for the last month. Carrie had mixed feelings about leaving the group. She had friends. She also wasn't sure she was leaving her supervisor under good conditions. She did not want to burn that bridge did not have to. Relationships have a way of coming back around.

Over the next few months Carrie gained greater practice and knowledge in her sales training broadening her book of business. She was given an internship opportunity in management to gain a more comprehensive experience. Such skills and experience helped both her and the organization. She began working as a relief supervisor in her department. She continued to work as a supervisor at two other part-time positions. Mike' firm continue to grow. Carrie's responsibilities advance with that.

3

Carrie worked that weekend to draft an initial plan. She received an email from Karen email and a reading list. Karen called this bio-mentoring. Karen explained that it is important to learn from those that have gone before. Many have spent a lifetime learning what you can learn from books and publications. Like face to face mentoring the time is well invested to shorten the learning curve. The reading list was long and distinguished. Karen also suggested a series of videos to challenge the way Carrie thought. Carrie was learning that knowledge is power though knowledge alone is not enough. Assessing and applications with continued assimilation builds the knowledge which builds the skills. When the skills improve, the experience advances. When the experience advances, the knowledge increases and the cycle continues.

One of the first books Carrie read on Sales was by a renowned sales trainer and motivational speaker. He told the story of a shoe company that sent a sales person to a remote developing country. The salesperson spent several weeks in the area talking to people and trying to get contracts. He sent a message home saying he was coming home because nobody bought shoes here. The company tried one more time sending their top sales person. The salesperson landed and spent a few days observing and talking with people throughout the country. He sent a message home sent an initial shipment of 100,000 units of common sizes and styles in different price points. Nobody owns shoes here. The market is ripe. The salesperson a month later asked that his sales team come as well. Over the next 12 months they sold over 4 million units. Perspective and being open to opportunities is a first step. See the need, create the need, and resolve the need. Carrie made notes.

Carrie studied communications and how to develop winning situations by solving a potential customers concerns. Blunt and blatant sales would have its time and place. She was learning her personality is not that direct but subtler. She understood asking questions with genuine concern and focus could make a difference but it would take time to develop her delivery. She began practicing immediately on the job. Sometimes her approach worked well. Many times, the results were dismal.

She emailed Karen after a particularly difficult day a month into the new position. Karen responded remember those that win the most have also lost the most. The home run kings are also the leaders in strikeouts. The top salesperson has likely received more no responses than any other team member at the organization.

Remember to always keep refining your approach. Carrie did and results gradually improved.

Carrie met with Karen monthly for coffee and teaching. Continually, Carrie improved and learned the tough lessons. Karen taught and asked the difficult questions to push Carrie a little more, just beyond her comfort zone. Little by little she shifted her thinking and results to make necessary changes in what was becoming a career decision with her company. Carrie began earning substantial bonuses that were a larger percentage of her paycheck and income flow. Her work with Michael's firm increased. She began training new employees in the call centers. She started mentoring new employees in orientation and during their probation.

Her next six months as a service team representative passed quickly in her group. The center director conducted her evaluation. She had worked with some of the best and brightest the company had to offer. The efforts and associations showed.

The director sat with Carrie. He reviewed her numbers. Carrie, how long have you been with the company. She replied almost 1.5 years. He smiled. What was your experience before coming here. She demurred. I worked at two fast food restaurants on the line. He smiled really. How have you learned this job so well? I have paid attention. I ask questions. I am blessed to work with a great team. I work with a few mentors. I am going to school also. I am in my second year of courses at the online university. Their expedited schedule and flexibility has really helped. He made some notes.

Carrie, what do you want to accomplish here and why? Carrie paused for a moment before answering. She replied, I would like to explore my options here. I have worked on your special project for almost six months. I have learned so much though I still have so much more to learn. I would like to continue advancing within the organization while I gain more experience. I am in the management training program for the organization as you know. In order to advance, I believe I will need to gain other experience.

The director smiled. Carrie, you are wise and have a keen eye. For someone as young as you are, you have a vision and a plan. I have spoken with the other directors as to those in the management program. As I selected you for this project and you have performed exceptionally, you have now been selected for a marketing internship period. You will no longer make commissions from the sales except those you made while in this group as long as they renew. You will begin working in developing marketing and signing new accounts as well as servicing old accounts assigned to you. You will begin as a specialist and gain leads after getting familiar with the process and products.

Carrie sighed. The director asked, are you not interested in the position? Carrie stated no, I am, though I would like to continue servicing my existing customers. I have a relationship built with many. The director asked do you think others cannot do a good job with your former customers. Carrie stated no, it is not that others would do fine. We are a tremendous organization with great people. I committed to my clients though and would like to continue serving them. You had stated when we started the project to commit to the best quality and provide the greatest continuity we can to our clients. I wish to continue this on.

The director stated, Carrie you can keep your old position if you wish. Sir, she replied, I would like to carry the vision forward and provide our customers the continuity of services and product offerings. I can likely make the continuous sales and upgrades as the relationship is continually built.

The director thought about this. She smiled knowing it is true the vision would continue for Carrie to service her customers. He chuckled. I will authorize this and pilot test this component with you. If you can maintain and improve your accounts while servicing your new and assigned accounts then okay. If the quality suffers on your current accounts, new and assigned accounts your director, myself, and you will revisit the issue. Is this understood. Carrie smiled. She stated clearly as long as I maintain the same compensations plans as my colleagues in these groups. The director agreed. Carrie would begin her marketing internship the next week. She serviced her accounts and informed them that she would be changing positions though would continue to provide them services. She encouraged them to reach out to her if she could answer questions and be of any service. She stated she would be in contact again in a few weeks. Please contact her at her email for the duration, she would be checking it regularly throughout the day. Customers responded in kind. Some thanked her for notifying them and not just dropping them.

4

The Marketing Department was two floors. Carrie arrived early and roamed the area. She started casual chats with a few people she knew by name but not by face. Most were struggling with Monday Blues and had no problem showing it. Carrie headed to a break room to sit, read, and observe before her meeting with the Director after she checked in with the Director's assistant.

The assistant came and walked her to the director's office at the appointed time. Carrie saw the frustration on so many. Most turned away and buried their heads in their work. Carrie thought about this. What did this mean?

She was escorted to the Director who greeted her warmly. It is great to have you here Carrie. Jim speaks so highly of you. So, you worked directly with him on his special project. What did you learn during that time. Carrie paused for a minute, then spoke carefully. I am honored to have the opportunity to expand my learning in this department. My time on the project allowed me to work with an elite team of professionals dedicated to the success of our team and the organization. I had little previous knowledge as to sales and communication.

The time on the team taught me much of what I know allowing me to refine my skills. The team was willing to risk and assert themselves at the possibility of failure, missing our goal, though that only happened one time. We sharpened each other, thereby exceeding our stretch goals. The power of a great team is exponentially stronger than a group of individuals assigned together. I would say as a final point, learn from each other. Learn the good, the bad, and the mediocre, then work together to overcome and continually improve.

The director nodded. Carrie, it sounds like you learned some good lessons on that team. I will be placing you under the tutelage of one of my top managers. She has a dynamic team. The team is working on their own special project and is shorthanded. Do you think you are up for the challenge? Carrie smiled. I hope so, I welcome the opportunity to learn and be challenged. The director smiled. Let me introduce you to her and we will get you started. Together they walked over to the manager Phyllis' office.

Phyllis was wrapping up her Monday team supervisor meeting. Harry, the director, introduced Carrie to Phyllis. He explained that Carrie would be in the group on a six-month internship for the Management Training program. Harry soon left to return to his office.

Phyllis welcomed Carrie to the group and asked about her experience. Carrie explained about her time in warranty services and logistics then onto the service center and to a special project in the inside sales team. Carrie and Phyllis talked about the marketing side from identifying a need, researching the need, designing a plan, then acting on the plan and assessing for continuous improvement. Carrie and Phyllis spoke about the unique arrangement of maintaining her previous accounts though 110% is expected in this position.

The company is investing seriously in you Carrie said Phyllis. Much is expected. To this point you have not disappointed. Be aware though taking on too much can lead to a rapid downfall. Carrie asked about training sessions and mentoring. Phyllis replied training is hard here. Most training is learned by doing. Watch those that have been doing the job for a while. Ask questions when it is appropriate learn what to do and what not to do. Study those who are successful, learn from those that are not.

Carrie, I have hand selected a mentor for you based on previous experience. I will warn you though. She is very good, very disciplined and will teach you well, though you must be reachable and willing to learn even when it does not make sense. You must be willing to get your hands dirty whatever the cost. Can you do that? Or, I can place you with someone that is very good and will teach you the finer points of marketing for your time here. Which would you prefer? Carrie smiled. I want to work for the mentor that will push me. Phyllis smiled and said wonderful. She walked Carrie over to Kamy.

Kamy was a distinguished, very professionally dressed woman probably in her late 40s. She carried herself with confidence. Kamy had finished her team meeting and was updating the results board. Phyllis introduced Carrie to Kamy. Kamy smiled and greeted her warmly. She asked a few pleasantries then got down to business.

So, Carrie, what do you want to learn while you are here? Carrie stated I want to gain a good understanding of how marketing works and how to excel in my work as to marketing. There is little I know in the field so I know I have a lot to learn. Kamy shook her head. I see, so you know little as to marketing. My teams work hard, work fast, and work together. We succeed together. We fail together. Thus, we support each other to improve individually and collectively. There is no I in team. I hear you insisted on keeping you clients from inside sales. While I can appreciate that, I will not have you sacrificing our team, our results to pad your paycheck. Carrie demurred for a bit then straightened up. Kamy, I have every intention of being quite loyal to the team, though I will expect the same courtesy. I may seek the wisdom of the team as to how I may serve my existing clients better while also serving my new clients and the existing clients I will be inheriting. Kamy smiled, okay you have some fire. I like that. You will need it.

Starting today you will sit with Jen and Sharon as to Marketing Sales and Service. I will be giving you your cases gradually over the next few weeks as you ramp up. Listen and pay attention these two ladies are incredible and are two of my top producers. They volunteered to mentor you. I want you to know that. I expect you will not waste their talents, or their time. Okay, alright, starting now you are on the team. Let me show you your desk. Your access has been given. The information is on your desk. I will introduce you to Jen and Sharon and you will be set. Carrie nodded. It was all happening so fast.

Carrie set her stuff at her desk pushed the on button of her computer when Jen and Sharon showed up at her desk. Kamy was standing outside the cubicle when they arrived. She introduced

Carrie they talked for about a minute and Kamy left. Jen and Sharon stepped inside the cubicle.

Jen turned to Carrie. Carrie, I hear you were doing pretty good over in sales on the project. Why would you leave that to come here? Carrie replied I am in the management training program. This is my rotation. I worked with some outstanding people on my team. I am looking forward to being a part of this team. Sharon said but you had established accounts, why start over? It is part of my getting a comprehensive training. I have a few accounts I am bringing with me to continue serving as a bit of a pilot program. I guess I am the lab rat in this case.

I want to learn marketing and how to be successful here. Sharon said stay away from the naysayers. Observe what they do then overcome the objection. If need be find an alternative way to achieve the objective. If the company does not have a clear path, develop one within your abilities. Know your resources. Jen and I are two resources.

Kamy is a great resource though know what specifically you want before you ask us to step up. We do not wobble very easily. Be clear and concise but ask questions for clarity if you do not understand. It is better you get it the first time. Carrie agreed.

Sharon said I have a few administrative things to take care of for a couple of hours. You will sit with Jen. I suggest take notes and watch her do her magic in service. This afternoon. You will sit with me for a few hours in sales. By then Kamy will be giving you files. You can review these and develop questions then about 3:30 the three of us will meet and wrap up the day. Agreed? They all nodded. Carrie put her computer in standby and left with Jen to sit with her.

5

The next several months proved very difficult though challenging. Carrie admittedly made many mistakes. She learned to work long hours often coming in early and staying late. She learned marketing, sales. and service well. She continued to maintain her previous accounts often being able to add services she learned about through marketing and her other contacts through different departments.

She asked her team for guidance and assistance in what came to be Wednesday Brown Bag sessions. Carrie, Jen, and Sharon started to address challenges as well as dealing with difficult customers. When the collective whole worked together tremendous potential was realized. It cost $1 and $50 from the bonus or 5% of the bonus which ever was less. The money went into a cumulative pot for a quarterly drawing. The first two pots were substantial equaling a few thousand dollars. Carrie won the second quarter pot.

Carrie continued to be mentored by Jen and Sharon though she quickly learned the job. She maintained and improved every account she had before coming in as well as those she was given in this group. When she began going to trade shows, she calendared a few remote days to meet personally with clients in their environment while maintaining her other work. Often at the end of the trip she came home with new contracts for existing clients and new clients she met along the way.

She adapted the policy of asking existing customers for three companies they would recommend her to for services. Her average was 2 out of the three adding her book of business. Her commute or free time she would jot notes of possible businesses to contact. She would do research on the companies before contacting them being informed as she presented, thus often walking away with a contract if only on a trial basis.

Carrie altered her appearance to look more of a young professional especially when at shows or meeting clients. She carried this to the office as well. She shared the bonuses with her team and with the clients that referred her and the referral signed. Her network grew exponentially during this time. She lost some customers try as she might. She tried referring them elsewhere to get them the best services to meet their described needs.

Carrie continued to read feverishly in whatever time she had. She had managed to make a few sales training conferences during this internship implementing much of what she learned continually refining and teaching others on her team, resulting in greater results for the team. She was a team member not an official leader.

She maintained regular contact with Karen. Karen encouraged her by short phone calls and notes. They exchanged emails as to progress in studies both formal and informal. They continued to meet the last Saturday 8am at their coffee bar.

Carrie had been asked out by a few young men at shows and conferences. She usually said no as work was calling and time was precious. She did begin several distance conversations to get to know each other better and assist each other. Most men fell away after a few months. Others excelled and advanced with her in their own companies. Most did not share the same drive and passion for their careers.

The work Carrie was doing with Michael had been stagnant as Michael had been experiencing some family issues. Carrie tried to help where she could. Her days between classes and work at both places were often in excess of 12 hours and often a weekend day partial day. She continued to average about 20 hours per week working in Michael's business either onsite or remotely, often making referrals.

The end of Carrie's internship in Marketing came. Harry, Phyllis, Kamy, Jen, and Phyllis all sat as a panel for her evaluation. Harry facilitated the panel. Jim had chosen to sit in on the evaluation as he had clients on the line as well due to the pilot project.

Harry asked Phyllis to review Carrie's performance. Phyllis summarized her assessment that Carrie had learned quickly, worked hard, and was a team player. She deferred to Kamy. Carrie had initiated with her mentors' steps to improve the team and to learn from the team through various interaction activities. She found ways to motivate and incentivize team members that had mediocre ratings, thereby raising collective results across the board.

Kamy looked at Jim. She maintained her accounts she carried over from inside sales. At first, we were concerned about this but she rose to the challenge often improving the accounts and bringing additional business to our group we otherwise would not have received. She improved her own accounts plus the ones we gave her and generated new accounts, some of which by her own initiative when she worked remotely. She improved interaction on her accounts. All while maintaining top marks in her classes. A note of concern. Carrie is working often 6 and 7 days per week an average of 12-hour days. There is a concern of burnout. Kamy deferred to Jen.

Jen stated Carrie was a pleasure to work with. She is a go-getter. We often had to tell her to slow down as it made the rest of us look bad. Carrie said she would not slow down but help the rest of us improve and work smarter if possible. She stated it was made very clear the team succeeds together and the team fails together. She knew setbacks would occur, though we are to learn from them and make the changes so as to win from them next time and the times after.

Sharon spoke up. She got excited about the trade shows and meeting with customers face to face again. Many of us had become complacent. She re-inspired us. She made the shows fun again. We added drawings and fun interaction games for prizes. Stuff we stopped years ago. She got our existing clients participating and brought in many leads making her presence and professionalism visible. She brought us together working as a team. It was not about her but about the collective team. We prospered together whether bonuses or business.

Carrie listened and smiled. The feedback had been mostly positive.

Harry summarized the evaluation. Carrie, I have worked for this organization for over 20 years. Most of my team has over 10 years working for me, including these fine young ladies here. I know how tough it is to please them, yet you have. This says so much for your character and your drive. As you bring this assignment to a close and prepare for your next internship there are some difficult decisions to make. You need to make them.

You have a choice in that you will move to the next phase which does not directly involve customer contact but serving in Human Resources in a satellite office. The purpose is one of the offices is experiencing some challenges and the Director of HR in the office has requested someone strong but willing to learn. You seem a natural fit. You can also choose to stay and either Jim or I are prepared to offer you a Supervisor position though you will gain us as mentors, you would terminate your management training program internship and accept a permanent position.

You may maintain your current client book of business, as well as begin making a small percentage of each team member you are assigned, as incentive to increase their books and the client's accounts. At 20 years old you are already making more than many colleagues twice your age just in commissions. If you choose to go to the internship, the same deal as before, no excuses for not doing the work expected and you are expected to maintain and improve your accounts. We will not expect you to increase the number of accounts, but increase the accounts you have.

Carrie asked where is the internship, will I have to relocate. It is in a remote office about 90 minutes from here. If I understand where you live it is about the same time to drive as what you do now, but in a different direction. These are tough choices.

Jim interjected. Carrie may I ask how are your parents? I know they were part of the reason you have done what you are doing. Carrie smiled. Thank you for asking Jim. My father is stronger and back working about 75% on light office duty. He is not earning his full pay yet. Mom is still working two full-time jobs to cover expenses. I give where and when I can. Jim asked, and school?

Carrie paused, it has been a difficult couple of sessions due to the travel and double duty working sales and marketing, but I am 3 classes from completing. I have applied for the executive MBA program, meaning if all goes well I should have my MBA in about 18-24 months from now. Jim nodded. Carrie, I would love to have you on my team as I know Harry would. It would allow things to normalize for you and allow you a little more of a life outside of the office.

Carrie thanked the committee. Almost 2 years ago I graduated high school not sure what my life would look like. I worked at 2 fast food places. My dad was mostly disabled. Mom worked her fingers to the bone and came home purely exhausted. I have done what I had to do to care for my family and my siblings.

Thank you to this organization and each of you for investing in me. Because of your investment, my dad is getting better. I am getting the education I wanted and thought I might never get. More so, I am blessed to have relationships and a network most professionals would dream to have, can have, but never choose to develop.

I am thankful for the opportunity to work for either Jim or Harry and your incredible organizations. I have my plan. I chose to commit to the management training plan. I committed to my education. I must stay true to myself and my plan. I will take the internship. Harry nodded and stated, excellent choice. While I am sorry for our loss, I am excited for you. I will make the arrangements. The Director of HR at the office will be reaching out to you in the next 24 hours to give you the particulars.

6

Carrie left for the weekend. She chose to drive up to the university her best friend from high school had transferred to after a year at the community college and working for a year. She left after work which had pretty much ended with her evaluation. The couple hour drive allowed her to think and assess.

She listened to her motivation playlist for part of the way. She made some notes as she drove. She stopped about 3/4 of the way to stretch, get some food and fuel. She checked her email. There was a message from her new Director Cassandra. She will call Carrie 7am at home on Monday. Please be in a quiet location where you can work. Please confirm. Carrie sent her confirmation, then continued her journey.

She arrived a few hours before her friend completed her shift at the pizza restaurant. Soon the friend, several friends, and fellow students began drinking, then drinking a lot. Carrie sat and talked with some of the students until the others were too drunk to engage in coherent conversation. She wondered if this was the college experience she had missed, yet not really. Most were not being responsible. She had matured past this in High School. This was not her life.

Saturday was not any better. Her friend slept late. When she and her roommates awoke they started drinking. Carrie pulled her laptop. She started doing some work and self-training. She read on her training while her friend and her friend's friends drank. The weekend was good for her and gave incredible perspective. She learned she had made some good choices though she was learning what the cost had been and the benefit she had gained.

Carrie considered the advantages of going off to college, enjoying a few years of relative freedom while taking courses and discovering what she wanted to do with her life. She and many others as she discovered would begin to work and take classes online or locally as they determined their path. Others chose to discontinue their formal academic education to get vocational training. All had advantages. All had disadvantages. Her path had brought her success and filled the need for her family.

She had been fortunate to meet some people willing to invest in her if she would invest in herself. Her life circumstances had forced her to eliminate some of these choices. While many of her friends from high school had chosen to work and take some classes though to no clear end goal, she had been given the opportunity to have a career and gain education and considerable experience.

Carrie, Sunday morning found a coffee house to get online and get a large cup of coffee. She knew her friend would not be up for a few hours. She opened her laptop and sipped her dark roast. She chatted with a few others in a more laid-back environment. As she read recent leadership and quality customer service articles, she made notes. A customer sitting near her noticed the article. She commented, excuse me do you read many of these articles. Carrie nodded, yes. I am studying leadership, sales, and service. The customer asked are you taking these courses at the university. Carrie shook her head. No, I am not. I do not go to school here. The customer replied, really? Where are you enrolled? Carrie stated I work full time for a global services company. Due to my schedule and other factors I go to school online.

The customer smiled. I find that very interesting. May I ask where you are enrolled. She told the customer. The customer asked that is very interesting. Are you taking leadership classes? Carrie responded in the affirmative.

The customer asked are you currently takin such a course. She said yes, I am in a business strategy. The customer asked may I inquire who your prof is? She stated I have Dr. Green. The customer smiled. The customer stated that is interesting. May I have your name? Carrie told him. He smiled I believe I am your professor Carrie. I am here doing my grading for the week and responding to discussions. Carrie, it is so nice to meet you.

Carrie smiled. Dr. Green, it is nice to meet you. I am up visiting a friend. I found out this weekend the experience is very different here. My friend has been drinking all weekend. I do not understand how this is beneficial. I work 40-70 hours per week while going to school full time. The professor stated you are gaining substantial experience while learning the academics your education is complimenting your experience.

They spoke for several minutes. Carrie logged into her classes. She headed back to her friends to have brunch before heading home. She arrived at the house of her friend to find her still passed out with the rest of the house. At 12:30 nobody stirred. She left a note for the friend that she got a call and had to get home. She would contact her in a few days. Carrie grabbed her stuff and started the drive home. She started thinking about her new position and her drive for advancement.

She was going to make the most of her opportunities. She would not have another college weekend like this one. She would create success, learn success, and teach success, as Karen had taught her. She set a goal. She set an income goal and a positional goal placing a date on them. At one point she pulled into a truck stop and documented several ideas, methods, and Plan, writing for almost an hour before continuing the journey home. She arrived late afternoon. She sat and watched a movie and had a pizza feed with her family that night. Tomorrow would be the start of a new drive in her career and school. She would continue on to greater opportunities.

7

Carrie woke early on Monday and went for her run, listening to motivational presentations and affirmations. As she neared the finish of her run, the morning mind fog had lifted. She prepared for her day. She made her coffee and headed to her room to await her new Director's call. Her parents would work with her siblings to keep the morning noise down.

At 7:00 straight up she received the call. Carrie listened as Cassandra explained that a box should have been delivered over the weekend with the instruction not to open until this morning. Carrie acknowledged that this had occurred. Cassandra told Carrie to go ahead and open the box, Carrie complied. Carrie found a two-inch binder, a current passport, and a thumb drive with a new laptop.

Cassandra explained that for the next few months Carrie would be traveling form location to location completing many of the HR tasks that had been allowed to pass but were causing concerns and disruptions in service. Cassandra explained that Carrie would have access to the company virtual private network. She would be able to access the employee database.

Carrie was advised be very careful making changes in the database. There are applications that need to be updated and confirmed in the database. Some paperwork may be a s simple as a signature that was missed, others may be an incomplete file. Cassandra stated you will work very independently. I am available if there are questions or concerns through email and text, call if absolutely necessary. I will monitor by the work completed at each location. I have a small team at corporate monitoring my field teams for accountability. The corporate team can also assist with travel, scheduling, and administrative if there is an issue. Each morning you will receive a report assessing the work from the day before.

You will always know where you stand. Any questions. Carrie said, no.

Cassandra stated, Carrie, I have heard good things about you. I also hear you are working long hours and have little social life. I am telling you, you will be traveling a lot. The job may challenge you in ways not previously thought of. Find ways to relax. To be honest I do not care when you get the work done as long as it is done on time or before and done right. If you work better at 2 am then work at 2 am. If you develop a system for the work to be done and it lessens your work time, that is fine. If it takes you 4 hours to complete what we schedule 8 hours that is fine, no worries. I do not ask for perfection, I do insist on excellence. I am giving you complete freedom with the understanding of what is expected and what is needed. You have additional work in caring for clients and accounts. You are expected to not only maintain but grow these accounts as no doubt has been explained. Are we clear? Carrie acknowledged.

Cassandra continued. Take today to get familiar with the laptop and its applications. Review the thumb drive as to what is there. You will be expected at the Monroe facility in the morning ready to go. Most places you can drive during this first month. You will begin flying probably next month. You will be gone most weekdays. I have included the account information to cover your travel and work expenses. These will be carefully monitored, and you will submit receipts through the scanner on your company phone and the software on the laptop. We also pay a stipend per mile below the federal governments allotted rate. You may want to keep a mileage log for us and for yourself to track mileage and expenses.

Cassandra asked any questions or concerns? Carrie stated no, she would familiarize herself with the equipment and be in Monroe tomorrow morning. Cassandra stated excellent, we will talk soon, and the call ended.

Carrie considered this call and what it might mean. She would have considerable freedom, more than she ever had before. She thought how do I best handle that? She stated, I am being trusted to do the work, that comes first, and play time is supplemental and could be a distraction. She mapped out a plan for Monroe and the other locations for the week. She began to get acquainted with the new systems. She began packing for the week as she would be traveling locally but not coming home due to distance. She shared with her family the descriptions of her new job. She was excited and a little nervous.

8

The next morning Carrie made the drive to the Monroe facility. When she arrived at 0600 the security guard let her in and escorted her to her assigned workspace for the day with her access badge. Carrie sat down at the desk and booted her laptop. She immediately went to company email. Cassandra was online. She immediately acknowledged Carrie.

Cassandra commented, Carrie you are an early worker, excellent. She stated, she too was an early worker. She worked half days, the question was more often which 12 hours would she work. Carrie replied, it is a sound work ethic. I am trying to make the bigger investment now to pay greater returns long term. Cassandra concurred this was a good path that worked well for many. Cassandra disconnected and Carrie went about her work.

Carrie reviewed the tasks for the day. She developed a plan for action to complete the work. Certainly, there would be disruption to the plan, thus she developed alternatives. Many of the personnel files were inaccurate or needed updating. All employees had been notified to review their profiles, acknowledge revisions and submit the changes. Carrie was there to audit files and obtain any missing information if needed. By 0730, Carrie had reviewed all the files and made a list of missing information. By 0800 she had scoured the systems for any missing information. Some of the information obtained led to other questions. She sent instant messages to all supervisors and managers to get the updates by 1000 as all employees in this office worked 8-5.

Carrie sent some emails and made some calls to clients. For the next hour she walked the halls getting to know some of the personnel casually as she familiarized herself with the office, the office culture and workplace environment. She monitored behaviors and studied the social groupings.

She walked into the break room and met Sharon. One of the colleagues in her initial call center training. She had become very disgruntled with the company. They talked for a bit. Carrie decided that was not a relationship she wanted. She headed back to her work area.

Carrie began updating the files. The audit was near complete. She had a few missing employees that had not responded. At noon. She sent an email that if the information was not received by 1600 a hold would be put on the employee's personnel file. Pay and work would be frozen until the information was provided. The order was authorized by Cassandra as all files must be brought current. The responses started coming in. Carrie stayed at her desk. She sent inquiries between email discussions. She wasted little time. A few workers tried to complain at her.

Carrie responded, three emails have been sent. We have the read receipts. A little personal letter has been sent to your home and your cubicle. A final email was sent this afternoon. Reasonable efforts and due diligence made including notifying your supervisor with each request. Noncompliance is now acted upon.

A few unkind words said. Carrie held her ground. A rough day. She made incredible potential with her works. She finished her day at Monroe and headed to her next site for tomorrow.

She made note of a few potential clients. She noted how she could help them. She formulated a contact letter to be sent. She noted addresses. Carrie would do some homework tonight. She hired an appointment setter to begin making focused efforts to advance her book. She made note for also advancing Michael's business and contacted him as to her current situation. He agreed to a commission structure for all business she brought in and serviced. Yes, this could be very lucrative indeed.

Over the next several months Carrie continued to refine her operations and her systems for making best use of available resources. Carrie refined her systems to make them more effective and efficient capitalizing on time, cost, and resources. She traveled throughout the nation and across the globe to the remote sites of the organization. She came to realize how different people are. The culture, and even the organization is significantly impacted by even minor shifts. She learned to adapt. Some of these lessons came at a high price. She made many mistakes, often learning from them as she went. Cassandra would meet with her for a few minutes most mornings as the majority of her team did not start until significantly later than Carrie chose to. Cassandra gave Carrie the extra time due to Carrie's added investment.

Carrie significantly grew her book of business as to sales and service within the organization as she travelled. She made very detailed notes as to each customer and organization that she serviced. She began to bring in more virtual assistants to make best use of her time and resources available. The book began to grow. She shared with her assistants a percentage of the profits. This would tend to give them more desired investment in the project as well as greater dedication and commitment to serving her over other clients.

Her efforts with Mike's organization also continued to grow substantially. She had greater freedom in this project than the organization in which she worked, which proved to be profitable for her. Carrie continued to refine her budding business systems. She realized quickly though, that the organization in which she worked allowed her the ability to serve both organizations without a conflict of interest as they were different industries offering different products and services.

Carrie understood that one organization was able to support the others. Often the other systems and organizations accentuated her abilities and resources for the one. She continued to assess how to improve in all areas. Karen was a large part of this process in her mentoring throughout this time. She began to talk to Cassandra about this as well in the way of personal management on a freelance basis.

Cassandra understood, as she owned multiple organizations in she which she could work virtually. She would contract for services with many different virtual organizations, using a virtual workforce giving greater control to her own. Carrie quickly learned to not assume complete loyalty, often people may have their own desires, agendas and concerns.

Know who you are talking to. Know the resources they offer. Know what you can offer them. Cassandra, Karen, Jim, and Harry all worked with Carrie to continue to build her book of business, continually improving it. Karen did advise Carrie that at some point a decision may have to be made as to what she would do with her future. Carrie did not fully understand what that meant.

Carrie during this internship and her travels completed her bachelor's degree. She enrolled in an executive MBA course that would allow her to continue to travel and work or participate remotely. She did change schools after doing some research.

She learned it was valuable to have a diverse education and portfolio of academic and practical knowledge works. The university's MBA program accepted several of her courses that expediting the process. Carrie's career was truly beginning to take off. Many of her friends were still sitting in in a classroom with no real experience and only conceptual knowledge.

Carrie throughout the six-month period was able to expand her business, clean up many of the HR issues that Cassandra was addressing in the organization, and grow her outside interests in order to diversify her income and potential. Cassandra offered Carrie additional work outside of her internship position in her own organization as she was very impressed with the work effort, the work ethic, and the results Carrie achieved in a short amount of time. She was willing to continue to mentor Carrie in these areas and growing her own organization. Karen agreed that this was advantageous to Carrie. These two mentoring opportunities would serve her well as she would get some very diverse and dynamic lessons and education from a practical standpoint.

Henry and Jim also offered their counsel and advice for expanding her book of business. They offered some additional outside resources and gave her some leeway as her book of business continued growing. Everybody one under this scenario won as the work did not suffer. Carrie's book of business was becoming too much for one individual. She had chosen wisely to begin to bring in other individuals for key aspects of these accounts. Some of which the organizations and departments committed resources and assistance. Others of which Carrie began to hire her own team based on the experiences and knowledge she had already acquired.

She did not need all sales people were or service people. Often, she needed good administrators that understood the dynamics of the systems as well as the importance of a strong back office. She needed good follow up representation in sales and service. She began to consult and contract pre-and post sales individuals that would be committed to her organization as she continued to bring in other contracts with organization such as Cassandra's and Mike's. She added service people to insure high quality service long after the sale and maintain a strong relationship as she continued to maintain contact with clients personally.

The internship came to an end and she understood it. Cassandra extended the internship to take a new position as a director of global human resources at the agency on a contract basis as Cassandra was given the contract for being the vice president of human relations to the organization. She knew Carrie had a very solid understanding of the organization and what needed to be done. She had trained up Carrie to take over this position as she would continue to promote. Having the right people in the right place doing the right work is a critical piece of any team.

During this time Carrie continued to grow her organization as well as those that she served. Her book of business was significant. While she did not hire the initial teams for the organization, she was beginning to get some practice in hiring new representatives and support teams throughout the organization with the resources that were available. Carrie, Cassandra, and Karen all agreed on a path to assist Carrie in growing and advancing teams, leadership, and results. The rubber met the road.

The basic training in foundations was over. Now it was time to build upon the foundation. Karen and Cassandra both taught Carrie in very different ways that it was at this time that most people feel that they would have the tools and resources but did not know what to do with them.

Having the information is only one piece of the puzzle. Knowing what to do with them and how to apply them makes the difference between success and something less. The teams prospered. Her organization prospered on all levels and with all that she worked with. She learned the good and the bad of hiring contractors. She learned the good and the bad of imbalance on a team and understanding the personalities and conflicts that can occur. She also learned the value of a sound workplace environment and work ethic to garner consistency and greater results.

As the year working with Cassandra wrapped up, Carrie took some time to reflect as to what were lessons she had learned what were results her team had achieved, and how did this time into her current plans. As the time grew near for the internship to end, Carrie would move to her next opportunity, Cassandra chose to meet Carrie personally for the first time. They met in the hotel restaurant outside San Francisco.

Cassandra and Carrie. shared a very nice dinner in which they discussed plans and objectives that had been achieved, and those yet unrealized. It was time for Carrie to move to a new position within the organization. Cassandra would stay on with her as a mentor but also as an advisor in her own organization. Carrie was building a sound advisory board for her own organization that had not yet officially taken shape. Cassandra spent some time talking to her about that. They talked about the trainings that Carrie had gone too. They talked about the books and articles read. They talked about the academic programs that Carrie completed. They laid out some goals. Though it was a long night it was a very prosperous night on all fronts.

That night Cassandra gave Carrie two envelopes and asked her not to open them until after the meeting was over and she was back in her room. Cassandra proved to be a very successful business woman in many ways. Carrie had learned a lot and had valued the experience, learning to listen more and talk less. She added value to expand the knowledge. Time was very valuable and very rare. It was by following this method that a greater and deeper respect was established for both parties. They parted as friends and business partners.

9

Carrie entered for hotel room for the evening. She sat down at her desk and the laptop booted up. Her tablet updated email and messages. Carrie opened the envelopes. In the first envelope was a check of a very substantial size. With the check was a letter and what appeared to be a contract. Cassandra stated in the letter that this was a bona fide job offer for Carrie to come to work with her for a two-year period and the check was a sign on bonus should she choose to do so. This would allow Carrie to learn new insight and possibilities while studying under Cassandra. She offered training, mentoring, and advancement opportunities to grow the organization.

Carrie was very flattered by the offer and opportunity as well as the size of the check. She put the envelope and the contents on the desk. She opened the second envelope. As she pulled the contents out there was a check. There was also another note. Cassandra had written if you have opened this envelope this check is a bonus from me to you for all your effort with the organization, and in advancing my own organization. If you have opened both envelopes, you are not sure if you want to take the offer in the first envelope.

I would invite you to consider this check as a bonus and what is at stake should you choose my contract or to continue with the organization. This is one of those times you must choose what is the right path for you, for now, and for the future. Both offer great opportunity, both will take you down very different path. Cassandra closed with I have enjoyed working with you, and I would consider it an honor if you would consider coming to work with me.

Carrie put the second envelope and its contents on the desk. She had much to consider. She put them aside for now in order to get the work done for the next few hours. She had been building her own organization. She knew she could advance Cassandra's house. Cassandra had more resources available to her. This would be an incredible learning opportunity. The organization was very good to her as well. They had incredible opportunities, advancement, and expansion potential. She could be a part of something tremendous. The third option, was she could be her own boss, something she would never consider two years ago.

At 20 years old running a large organization and expanding her services to other organizations because she had something unique to offer. This was something that most 20-year-olds did not understand. She continued to do her work. She made the contacts that she needed to make. She reached out to companies and researched their profiles to determine how she and her organizations could best serve these potential clients. It was about understanding the power of a network in the power of many versus the power of one trying to do the work of many.

A few hours into her work, she fell asleep at her desk considering the offers and opportunities of what was to come. A couple of hours later she woke, and prepared to go to bed before starting her day. She reviewed her messages and there was an email from Cassandra using the organization email. She opened it and it stated tomorrow morning at 8 AM you will receive a phone call from your new director at the organization. It was at that point you will get your next performance evaluation as you have completed the segment of the internship. Carrie, I wish you the very best in whatever you decide. Carrie contemplated that email and then fell on the bed to sleep.

## 11

Early the next morning Carrie awoke to her mobile phone vibrating. She found a reminder message to meet her Director in the hotel coffee shop at 8 instead of a call. The message was from Karen. She got up and put herself together. She headed down to the coffee shop. Karen was in the back booth against a far wall.

Carrie walked back to the booth, greeting Karen. Karen invited her to join her. Karen stated they would be joined by a few others today.

Carrie wondered what this was about. Was this her mentoring session, her evaluation, or meeting her new director, or something else? Carrie ordered a coffee and fruit plate.

Carrie and Karen spoke about the past few weeks and what had happened. Carrie had continued to grow her business, Mike's business, Cassandra's business as well as that of the organization. Carrie had been very busy.

Carrie, I am doing something a little different here, I find myself in slightly unchartered waters. Karen continued. You know me as a representative within Human Resources and as a trainer for the organization. The information is true though not completely. Carrie looked up. Jim, Cassandra, and Harry were standing next to the booth. Karen invited them to sit. Karen greeted each, then continued. Carrie, I have not been completely honest with you.

I will often do the customer service training because to me this is the bread and butter of the organization. Being able to communicate the organization to the customer, creating a winning situation is essential to the core of the organization. To this end, if we do not do this, we lose customers past, present, and future. I teach the essentials over a several day session as it serves to see who is in our organization and how they interact. As the trainer, I get to know at a deeper level each of the trainees.

You were so young and inexperienced when you entered the training almost 2.5 years ago. I was not sure if you would make it. You aligned with some interesting choices. You might be interested to know that you are the only person from that training class still with the organization. You are known by the company you keep. You are known by those in whom you associate and maintain relations with.

I agreed to mentor you and really was not sure you would stick with it. You were young with family problems. The odds were not stacked in your favor. You persisted. You enrolled in college, completing a bachelor degree within 2.5 years. You are now into your MBA. Congratulations! You have been in the management training program for 2.5 years and have excelled. You might like to know. You have the second highest performance rating ever in the program over the past 30 years. Carrie smiled.

Carrie, you are accomplished. You have achieved a great deal. You exceeded many expectations. You continue to thrive. You challenged the policies and processes producing at an incredible level for your clients and each of your assignments.

You never gave up your book of business and continued to maintain and improve the relationships. I understand you have had job offers to draft you away from the organization. I understand also you are developing your business as well as that of a Fabrication shop in your home town. Based on the reports Mike's business has grown by over 400% in the past 18 months due to a contract he has with you. Carrie smiled though looked a little confused.

Karen chuckled slightly. Carrie did you think you were being stealthy? Carrie smiled, no, though I did not think I was being blatant either. Karen smiled, no you were not blatant. If we had thought you were being conflicted or double standard, it would have been addressed. The truth is we, she motioned to all at the table, have been watching you. You have been tested. You have been measured. You have been found successful. Carrie stated this is all well and good. I am not clear as to what is happening right now.

The group chuckled slightly. Karen stated Carrie in many ways the past two years plus have been a test for you. Each of us are successful entrepreneurs. A network of entrepreneurs. We work together to benefit each other. By serving the needs of others we meet our own goals. I own the organization. I am the only person in the organization history that tested better than you in the program. My predecessor ran a tight, but very different ship than I do.

He too invested in a young girl with no real experience or knowledge. Two years later, I had offered to buy the company. He had a family situation that would require he sell. We structured a deal for me to purchase at a small upfront price as a junior owner and over the next five years continue to grow the business. In five years he would become the junior owner for another five. I would be the senior and majority owner, then eventually the sole owner. I did not have to carry paper and the business grew exponentially. Jim, Harry, and Cassandra have similar stories.

What you do not know is you not only grew my business but massively grew each of theirs. Mike walked up to the table. Carrie smiled. Karen chuckled. Yes, Mike is also part of our group. You also grew his business. What is further interesting is that while doing all this and working on your education, you built your own substantial business. I see you are making good money yet all the money you have made, you live tasteful but simply. You seem to do nothing with it. You do not maintain employees though have many contractors. Why is that? Carrie demurred a little sheepishly.

Karen, you have been a great mentor. She looked around. You have all been great mentors. I have learned so much from you. I am so blessed to have you as my friends as well as really my advisory council of sorts, whether you knew you were or not. The truth is as you stated my family was struggling. My dad was sick and unable to work. My mom worked 2 jobs. My siblings worked where they could. It was my job though and the organization that kept my family going. Each of you contributed to getting my family strong again. I have invested in my family. Karen smiled. That makes sense.

Karen continued. Carrie, let's get to it. The organization is essentially a large, massive and diverse network of companies. Many of us run multiple companies. I have been serving as the Chief Operating Officer for the past five years. I would like to move back to my board position with the others seated here. You have literally been in a 2.5-year job interview.

She pulled an envelope and slid it over to Carrie. Carrie opened the envelope. There was a one-page contract. Carrie began to read.

We the board of The Organization extend to you the opportunity to serve as Chief Operations Officer and President of The Organization. Salary is commensurate to performance. There is no predetermined salary. You will be paid 8% of net profits with an expense account to not surpass 2% of net to cover housing, travel, and transportation. Performance bonuses are conditional to surpassing of The Organization board expectations of a minimum 10% entrepreneurial growth and ROI growth to achieve a minimum 18% annually. You will run The Organization in conjunction with The Organization's vision and mission within the structures that are pre-established. You are free to work your own businesses, expanding and growing your enterprises as long as the minimums of your contract at The Organization are met.

You are free to use The Organization resources for capital, expansion, and growth, though The Organization is to be fairly compensated as we all drink from the same well. The six of us all share the same 8% net each. The remainder is reinvested into the organization. By signing below, you agree to these terms.

Carrie looked up. Are you sure. I am only 20. I will be 21 in a month. You want me running your company conglomerate. Karen smiled. Carrie, you already have been for the most part. You are smart and experienced and are producing a tremendous potential.

Cassandra stated, Carrie, my offer still stands to work in my organization as well. It is not an either-or situation. The bottom line is you cannot and will not do it alone. We have faith in you. We have invested in you. Come join us. We are each offering additional consulting fees as we collect from each other.

Carrie smiled. Well, as you have not completely told me the truth until this morning if I am to do this I need to let you know, I too have not been completely honest. Karen asked what do you mean?

I said I have been investing in my family. While this is true, maybe not in the way you have been thinking. When I was offered the training class and after first speaking with Karen and her agreeing to mentor me, I did my own experiment at the advice of my uncle a corporate attorney and my aunt an investment advisor. I incorporated. I paid myself a salary of $1000 each month. I lived at home, having no real expenses except clothes for work and gas or maintenance for my car, this amount has been more than sufficient. The rest has been placed into capital funds and an investment portfolio.

For the past year my father and mother have been able to work drawing a significant and reasonable wage working in my startup companies. My dad's medical bills are mostly paid. He runs my insurance and financial services office with my aunt as the Principal Advisor. My mother has gone into real estate and property management getting her license. We fix and flip properties as well as provide clean reasonable housing to the disadvantaged, this way we are helping others. We own several rentals we were able to purchase smart through ongoing creative financing options, solving previous owners' problems.

My sister operates a small mobile check cashing and micro loan business we started for young entrepreneurs. The business has been quite lucrative. In addition to my sales teams that produce a significant income and will be further developed, I recently started a small virtual assistant contracting firm, subcontracting my contractors for a percentage of the take. Everybody wins. I keep everyone working and producing. As of last night, and with Cassandra's generous offer we negotiated, I will be able to now fund my purchase of a regional master franchise license for a small sandwich shop enterprise.

Hopefully, the next few months I will begin selling unit franchises and providing the training needed. I have also begun a training and development firm, mostly solo-preneur for speaking and training engagements online and the occasional live event. I have friend of mine I went to high school with that is a junior in college as an English major ghost writing my first motivational teaching book.

The other board members chuckled and smiled saying there really is a lot more to you isn't there? Carrie smiled. I listened to those who knew. I acted on that which I believed. I lost some. I gained more. We invested in each other. My family took care of each other. We are stronger than ever. My brother will begin training at the sandwich franchise corporate center to be a general manager of our first business unit. We take care of each other as you each took care of me. The team applauded and congratulated her. She was exactly what they wanted. She signed the contract. They were now all in business together.

Karen slid one more envelope over to Carrie. Carrie opened the envelope. Carrie, Karen said as a junior member of our team the past year, we agreed to pay you a 4% net minus salary paid, for the past 2.5 years. You made us a lot of money expanding many of our operations and reminding us each of what is possible when we invest in others, build systems, and build the relationships. Carrie opened the envelope. She stared at it for what seemed to her like 20 minutes and was maybe 30 seconds. She had never seen such a large amount on one check before. She smiled. I know just what to do with it. They all laughed. Jim chuckled based on what you just told us, I do not doubt it.

The board sat for another hour telling stories of the experience and drinking bad hotel coffee. By mid-morning they had all dissipated to their different enterprises getting back to work. Carrie checked out and headed home to her family.

## Epilogue

The next two years Carrie developed special relationship teams to build and implement the power of relationship she continually reinforced that in the days of the global and ever-advancing technology based economies. Customers past, present, and future all have many choices. If we do not stand out to them as someone unique and extraordinary, they will go where they will be made to feel special. We will be extra ordinary and run with the flock of everyone else's. The Organization adopted a soaring eagle as its mascot symbolizing the potential to soar to incredible heights.

The Organization through continuous strategic development and execution grew exceeding 25% per annum. The start of year 3 they were on track for a massive, highly leveraged expansion of over 40% based on a 20% investment into related markets investing in vertical and horizontal integration. The Organization was growing dynamically.

## Afterward

Carrie. The young 25-year-old trainer walked into the training room. She had laid out all the manuals. She took a sip of coffee. She liked around the room. In the back of the room, was a shy, timid, and reserved young teenage woman. She was trying to be invisible. Carrie smiled to herself. She walked over to the young lady and said "Hello, I am Carrie. I will be your trainer "


The End.

The Team Development process:

- Be Open to possibilities
- Be Teachable
- Learn by doing
- Develop Mentor Relationships
- Expand your learning
- Learn different areas
- Ask Questions, Take Notes, Review
- Risk
- Power of Many vs The Power of One
- Power of the Acorn
- Build the Support Team
- Network
- Teach what you know, Train others
- Teach others to train others
- Repeat

## Ten Steps to building a Team

1. Have a product you believe in
2. Commit to the Product
3. Commit to the Organization
4. Decide to Decide
5. Find a Mentor
6. Learn, Grow, Read
7. Practice, Fail, Improve, Repeat
8. Build your Support System
9. Teach Others
10. Teach Others to Teach Others

Books by Coach Dr. JAG:

The Core 4 Life Management System

The Core 4 Life Management System workbook.

Foundations in Coaching

The Coaching Manual.

WAH and Other Lame Excuses

The Purge

Implementing the Leader Relationship

Investing in Wealth Building: The Journey from Penny to Wealth

Investing in Wealth Building: The Journey from Penny to Wealth Workbook

Social Media Stimulation: 10 Powerful Tips for Social Networking Success

Climb any Mountain

The Power of the Acorn: A lesson to grow your organization

The Parable of the Diner: A lesson on community

When Good Credit Goes Bad: A story of building solid credit